© 2002 by Barbour Publishing, Inc.

1-58660-430-9

Cover art © Corbis, Inc.

Interior illustrations by Todd Smith.

All rights reserved. No part of this publication may be reproduced or transmitted by any form or by any means without written permission of the publisher.

All Scripture quotations are taken from the HOLY BIBLE, NEW INTERNATIONAL VERSION®. NIV®. Copyright © 1973, 1978, 1984 by International Bible Society. Used by permission of Zondervan Publishing House. All rights reserved.

Scripture quotations marked KJV are taken from the King James Version of the Bible.

Published by Barbour Books, an imprint of Barbour Publishing, Inc., P.O. Box 719, Uhrichsville, Ohio 44683, http://www.barbourbooks.com

Printed in China.

World's Best Daddy

KELLY KOHL AND KATHRYN SHUTT

World's Best Daddy

Why God Made Fathers

God knew that each one of us would need
Shelter and guidance
Throughout all our growing-up years,
Warmth and compassion for all of our problems
And strength for our worries and fears. . . .

He saw that we needed wisdom for living,
A knowledge of heaven above,
True understanding of life's deeper meanings,
Examples of kindness and love.

And so He made fathers to stand by our side,
To inspire us in every endeavor,
Whose faith and devotion will last through our lives
And whose love we will cherish forever.

AUTHOR UNKNOWN

Introduction

You are receiving this little book because, from a "little" perspective that means "a lot," you are the world's best daddy. Out of all the fathers in the world, you were hand-picked by God to love and care for your child. . .and to guide him or her into adulthood.

Enjoy the quotations, stories, prayers, and poetry throughout—all of which will remind you of the special role you play in your child's life. And cherish the unique fill-in and coloring pages your child has completed especially for you. This is a treasured keepsake in honor of you—the world's best daddy!

World's Best Daddy

He that raises a large family does, indeed,
while he lives to observe them,
stand a broader mark for sorrow;
but then he stands a broader mark
for pleasure, too.
BENJAMIN FRANKLIN

A father's Love

As arrows are in the hand
of a mighty man;
so are children of the youth.
Happy is the man
that hath his quiver full of them.
PSALM 127:4–5 KJV

World's Best Daddy

When Mike's first child was born, his ultimate goal was to be a great father to his son. He wanted his son to love and respect others. . .and to love God above all.

When his son began to show a strong will of his own, Mike knew that he had to discipline his child when he did wrong. It was so hard to break his little one's heart. Mike knew, though, if he didn't show Jared right from wrong, he would never learn to obey.

Every time Mike had to correct Jared, he always spoke the words, "I love you, Son. But you must learn to obey Daddy." Then he would hold him until his tears subsided.

This kind of love is a mirror image of God's love to us—His children. God demands our obedience, but when we sin, His love for us never wavers. He is always there to pick us up and hold us lovingly in His arms.

As a father has compassion on his children,
so the LORD has compassion on those who fear him.
PSALM 103:13

. . .

I do not love him because he is good, but because he is my little child.

RABINDRANATH TAGORE,
The Crescent Moon

. . .

Be kind to thy father, for when thou wert young,
Who loved thee so fondly as he?
He caught the first accents that fell from thy tongue,
And joined in thy innocent glee.
MARGARET COURTNEY

World's Best Daddy

This is how I love spending time
with you, Daddy. . .

World's Best Daddy

It is a wise father that knows his own child.
WILLIAM SHAKESPEARE

. . .

Blessed indeed
is the man who hears
many gentle voices
call him father!
LYDIA M. CHILD

World's Best Daddy

Thank you for being a strong example of Jesus' love, Daddy.

World's Best Daddy

Dear Lord,

Thank You for this little life that You have entrusted to my care. Please give me strength and guidance in raising my child. May I always reflect Your loving Spirit, so my child can see Your love through me.

Amen.

World's Best Daddy

What Makes a Dad

God took the strength of a mountain,
The majesty of a tree,
The warmth of a summer sun,
The calm of a quiet sea,

The generous soul of nature,
The comforting arm of night,
The wisdom of the ages,
The power of the eagle's flight,

World's Best Daddy

The joy of a morning in spring,
The faith in a mustard seed,
The patience of eternity,
The depth of a family need.

Then God combined these qualities.
When there was nothing more to add,
He knew His masterpiece was complete,
And so He called it. . .Dad.

AUTHOR UNKNOWN

World's Best Daddy

Children are poor men's riches.
ENGLISH PROVERB

. . .

It doesn't matter
who my father was;
it matters who I
remember he was.
ANNE SEXTON

. . .

My son, despise not the chastening of the LORD;
neither be weary of his correction:
For whom the LORD loveth he correcteth;
even as a father the son in whom he delighteth.
PROVERBS 3:11–12 KJV

World's Best Daddy

I love you, Daddy, because. . .

_____

_____

_____

_____

_____

_____

_____

World's Best Daddy

The History of Father's Day

Mrs. John B. Dodd, who wanted a special day to honor her father, William Smart, is credited with first proposing the idea of a "father's day." Mr. Smart was left to raise six children alone when his wife died in childbirth. He lived on a farm in eastern Washington State.

The observance of the first Father's Day occurred on June 19, 1910, in Spokane, Washington. Although Mrs. Dodd had wanted the celebration to take place on the first Sunday in June (her father's birthday), the Spokane council couldn't get the resolution through the first reading until the third Sunday. In various towns and cities, others were also beginning to celebrate a "father's day."

President Calvin Coolidge was the first president to support the idea of a national Father's Day, though it was President Lyndon Johnson who signed a proclamation declaring the third Sunday in June as Father's Day.

World's Best Daddy

The Father's Day Flower

The official flower for Father's Day is
the rose—red or white.
Under the suggestion of Mrs. Dodd,
a white rose represents a father who is deceased
and red for a father who is living.

World's Best Daddy

Here's a fun Father's Day tie that I colored just for you, Daddy.

World's Best Daddy

Children's children are
the crown of old men;
and the glory of children
are their fathers.

PROVERBS 17:6 KJV

World's Best Daddy

Being a good daddy is. . .

World's Best Daddy

The Prodigal Son
LUKE 15:11–32

Jesus continued: "There was a man who had two sons.

"The younger one said to his father, 'Father, give me my share of the estate.' So he divided his property between them.

"Not long after that, the younger son got together all he had, set off for a distant country and there squandered his wealth in wild living.

"After he had spent everything, there was a severe famine in that whole country, and he began to be in need.

"So he went and hired himself out to a citizen of that country, who sent him to his fields to feed pigs.

"He longed to fill his stomach with the pods that the pigs were eating, but no one gave him anything.

"When he came to his senses, he said, 'How many of my father's hired men have food to spare, and here I am starving to death!

" 'I will set out and go back to my father and say to him: Father, I have sinned against heaven and against you.

World's Best Daddy

" 'I am no longer worthy to be called your son; make me like one of your hired men.'

"So he got up and went to his father. But while he was still a long way off, his father saw him and was filled with compassion for him; he ran to his son, threw his arms around him and kissed him.

"The son said to him, 'Father, I have sinned against heaven and against you. I am no longer worthy to be called your son.'

"But the father said to his servants, 'Quick! Bring the best robe and put it on him. Put a ring on his finger and sandals on his feet.

" 'Bring the fattened calf and kill it. Let's have a feast and celebrate.

" 'For this son of mine was dead and is alive again; he was lost and is found.' So they began to celebrate.

"Meanwhile, the older son was in the field. When he came near the house, he heard music and dancing.

"So he called one of the servants and asked him what was going on.

World's Best Daddy

" 'Your brother has come,' he replied, 'and your father has killed the fattened calf because he has him back safe and sound.'

"The older brother became angry and refused to go in. So his father went out and pleaded with him.

"But he answered his father, 'Look! All these years I've been slaving for you and never disobeyed your orders. Yet you never gave me even a young goat so I could celebrate with my friends.

" 'But when this son of yours who has squandered your property with prostitutes comes home, you kill the fattened calf for him!'

" 'My son,' the father said, 'you are always with me, and everything I have is yours.

" 'But we had to celebrate and be glad, because this brother of yours was dead and is alive again; he was lost and is found.' "

Lord, *May I always remember this story when my child goes astray. . .and always readily forgive my wayward child, as You readily forgive Your children. Amen.*

A Father's Calling

Fathers, do not exasperate your children;
instead, bring them up in the training
and instruction of the Lord.

EPHESIANS 6:4

World's Best Daddy

A Father's Responsibility

God's plan for you was to be a father—what a high calling, to have a child looking up to you with awe and wonder. God wants you to teach your child by example. Show your child the strength that can be found in God's Word. . .and the unceasing comfort that the Lord provides for His children.

When you're unsure of how to handle a situation or how to deal with your child, just ask yourself one question—"What would Jesus do?"—and you won't go wrong.

Good Advice for Fathers:

Do all the good you can,
By all the means you can,
In all the ways you can,
In all the places you can,
At all the times you can,
To all the people you can,
As long as ever you can.
JOHN WESLEY, *Rules of Conduct*

World's Best Daddy

The most important thing
a father can do for his children
is to love their mother.
DAVID O. MCKAY

. . .

Life affords
no greater responsibility,
no greater privilege,
than the raising of
the next generation.
C. EVERETT KOOP

. . .

I cannot think of any need in childhood
as strong as the need for a father's protection.
SIGMUND FREUD

World's Best Daddy

I'm glad that you're my daddy, because. . .

World's Best Daddy

A good man leaveth an inheritance
to his children's children:
and the wealth of the sinner is laid up for the just.
PROVERBS 13:22 KJV

. . .

The just man walketh
in his integrity:
his children are
blessed after him.
PROVERBS 20:7 KJV

World's Best Daddy

You make me
feel safe, Daddy.

World's Best Daddy

You know you're a dad when you say things like. . .

- Don't ask me; ask your mother.

- You didn't beat me. I let you win!

- A little dirt never hurt anyone. . . . Just wipe it off.

- I told you. . .keep your eye on the ball.

- Turn off those lights. Do you think I'm made of money?

- We're not lost. I'm just not sure where we are.

- No, we're not there yet.

World's Best Daddy

- As long as you live under my roof, you'll live by my rules.

- I'm not sleeping—I was watching the show on that channel.

- I'm not just talking to hear my own voice!

- In my day. . .

- Eat it! It will grow hair on your chest!

- If your friend jumped off a bridge, would you?

- As long as you tried your hardest, that's all that matters.

AUTHOR UNKNOWN

> ## World's Best Daddy

Proverbs 4:1—9,
A Father's Wisdom—

"**Listen,** my sons, to a father's instruction; pay attention and gain understanding.

"I give you sound learning, so do not forsake my teaching.

"When I was a boy in my father's house, still tender, and an only child of my mother, he taught me and said, 'Lay hold of my words with all your heart; keep my commands and you will live. Get wisdom, get understanding; do not forget my words or swerve from them. Do not forsake wisdom, and she will protect you; love her, and she will watch over you. Wisdom is supreme; therefore get wisdom. Though it cost all you have, get understanding. Esteem her, and she will exalt you; embrace her, and she will honor you. She will set a garland of grace on your head and present you with a crown of splendor.' "

World's Best Daddy

F . . . You are my friend.

A . . . You are my ally.

T . . . You are my teacher.

H . . . You are my hero.

E . . . You are my example.

R . . . You are my rock.

You are all these things
and more, Daddy!

World's Best Daddy

Daddy, thank you. . .

- for praying for me every day.

- for providing for all my needs.

- for loving me unconditionally.

- for picking me up when I fall down.

- for tucking me in at night.

- for taking me to church so I can learn about Jesus and His love for me.

Thank you for being YOU!

World's Best Daddy

Dear Lord,

It's frightening to think that I must bring my child up in a world where nothing is guaranteed—nothing but Your love, Lord. May I always be a shining example to my child and show her that she can depend on You always. For we can never be separated from Your love. . .even when it seems at times that our entire world is falling apart. Thank You, Lord, for Your unconditional love.

Amen.

World's Best Daddy

Here's a picture I drew just for you, Daddy.

World's Best Daddy

Here are some things I promise to do for you this week to show you that I appreciate you, Daddy.

World's Best Daddy

Happy Father's Day! You are the World's Best Daddy! I LOVE YOU!